Hike Myles Standish State Forest!
Thirty hikes among the Ponds and Pines of Myles Standish State Forest in Plymouth and South Carver, MA.
By Frank Werny

Hike Myles Standish State Forest!
Thirty hikes among the Ponds and Pines of Myles Standish State Forest in Plymouth and South Carver, MA.
By Frank Werny

Disclaimer
As in other hiking books, the information in this book is meant as a guide only. The author cannot be responsible for the conditions of the trails, for the safety of the trails, the accuracy of the maps, for anything that happens while you are using the trails, or for the continued accessibility of the trails. The introduction includes some advice, but following that advice also is not sufficient to guarantee a safe hike or walk. Use common sense, make adequate preparations, and take proper precautions during the hike.

Printed in the United States of America
Published by On Blueberry Hill Press
First Edition July 2015

Text by Frank Werny
Cover Design by Cover Creator and Frank Werny
All photos and trail maps by Frank Werny unless otherwise noted
Cover photo taken at Wing Hole, MSSF

ISBN-13: 978-1514171950

ISBN-10: 1514171953

Please direct comments or corrections to frankwerny@gmail.com

On Blueberry Hill Press
Plymouth, MA
frankwerny@gmail.com

.

Additional books are available at www.createspace.com/5535128
Or frankwerny@gmail.com or **www.amazon.com**

Other books also available:

Hike Plymouth and Beyond! Latest edition 2013. Over100 hikes in and around Plymouth. In full color.
www.createspace.com/4403063

Hike Plymouth!
Over 70 easy hikes in and around the Plymouth, MA, area. In full color.
www.createspace.com/3586892

Frank Werny

'Walks among the Pines and Ponds of Plymouth and Surrounding Areas'.
Over 70 easy hikes in and around the Plymouth, MA, area. Black and white.
www.createspace.com/3399738

Please also contact me if you find that trails have changed or with other comments
you might have.
frankwerny@gmail.com

Acknowledgements
 I would like to acknowledge the help I received from members of Friends of Myles
Standish Forest, the many hikes I enjoyed with them, and their efforts in staging
hikes and many other events in MSSF. Specifically I would like to thank John
Bescherer and Malcolm McGregor for taking me on trails in areas of the forest that I
was not familiar with.
"Friends of Myles Standish State Forest (FMSSF) is organized to promote and
conserve the natural, scenic and historical resources of Myles Standish State Forest
(MSSF) and its Satellite Areas; to foster the use and enjoyment MSSF by the public
in a manner consonant with the protection and preservation of the environment; to
engage in such educational, scientific and charitable activities as will assist the
Commonwealth of Massachusetts in the operation of MSSF."
http://www.friendsmssf.com/aboutus.html

Myles Standish State Forest
Headquarters
Cranberry Rd., S. Carver, MA
508 866-2526

Hike Myles Standish State Forest

Myles Standish State Forest (MSSF)

Myles Standish State Forest is a state forest located in Plymouth and South Carver in southeastern Massachusetts, approximately 45 miles (70 km) south of Boston. There are great trails thorough the Pine Barrens by many beautiful ponds, kettle ponds, bogs and valleys. It is the largest publicly owned recreation area in this part of Massachusetts and is managed by the Department of Conservation and Recreation (DCR)[1].

The forest is part of the Atlantic Coastal Pine Barrens ecoregion and consists largely of pitch pine and scrub oak forests—at 26 square miles (67 km2), one of the largest such forests north of Long Island. The forest surrounds 16 lakes and ponds, including several ecologically significant coastal kettle ponds. The Plymouth red-bellied turtle, an endangered species population found only in this area, exists in about twenty of the ponds of the state forest and the adjacent Massasoit National Wildlife Refuge. The shores of these kettle ponds are extremely sensitive to trampling. Please observe the barriers and signs posted indicating sensitive areas and respect the unique natural qualities of the park. Many miles of hiking trails take visitors deep into the forest.[1]

No off-road vehicles allowed. Hunting is allowed during the season, and two Wildlife Management Areas within the forest are stocked with game birds in October and November. Some of the ponds are also stocked. In the summer, interpretive programs, such as pond shore walks and cranberry bog explorations help acquaint visitors with the unique natural, cultural and historic aspects of the state forest.[2]

It is easy to explore and there are many places to discover. In addition to the trails on the MSSF maps and in this book there are many trails not shown on any map. So be careful not to get lost. You might keep in mind between which of the forest roads you area hiking at any one time. On most of the trail maps in this booklet "Google earth" will show in the south-east corner

Thirty hikes are included here. They are not necessarily the same as the MSSF Forest Service maps nor are they in any way endorsed by them. They are based on personal hikes and have no official standing. I strongly advise getting a latest forest map at MSSF headquarters to supplement the ones in the book. When trails are marked single marks indicate to continue in that direction. Double marks indicate that a change in direction is coming up. The top mark is displaced in the direction of the turn. Many of the trail maps will have a small N in the upper right hand corner indicating north.

I should also point out that due to ever changing conditions the author cannot be responsible for the accuracy of the content of the book nor the safety of the trails. You should use the book as a guide and always proceed with caution. Trails change, weather conditions affect footing, the Forest Service may put up signs, etc. Specifically, the State Forest has been removing large quantities of dead red pines. To do this they drove large equipment into the forest and generated new "roads". These can obliterate trails.

1. http://www.mass.gov/eea/agencies/dcr/massparks/region-south/myles-standish-state-forest.html
2. Wikipedia, http://en.wikipedia.org/wiki/Myles_Standish_State_Forest

Resources:
The maps produced were prepared using a Garmin eTrex Venture HC GPS unit and
Garmin WayPoint and were overlaid on MassGiss using the Google Earth software.
In addition some historical and location information was taken from Wikipedia[1] on
the internet.

Hikes in MSSF

Distribution of hikes in Myles Standish State Forest

Hikes in Miles Standish State Forest:

MSSF Hikes Frank Werny		Miles	Page
A. Central			
Around College Pond 1	Central	5.1	11
Around College Pond 2	Central	4.5	12
Bentley Loop	Central	4	14
Central MSSF & Fire Tower	Central	4.2	16
Cherry Pond Valley Trail	Central	2.8	18
Fire tower to Torrey Pond	Central	3	20
Three Cornered Pond Loop	Central	4.1	22
East Head Reservoir from HQ	Central	2.6	24
East head Reservoir From P2	Central	5.2	26
B. West			
NW Corner	West	3.8	28
Little Widgeon Pond	West	2.5	30
Curlew Pond Loop	West	3	32
Federal & Rocky Pond	West	4.8	34
Around Federal Pond	West	4.8	36
Lost Horse Bog	West	5.2	38
Shady Acres	West	6.5	40
Barrett Pond Loop	West	3	42
Eq Lot P3 to Grady Pond	West	2.9	44
C. South			
Charge-Fearing Pond Area	South	4.7	46
Charge Pond Loop	South	5.2	48
Cutter's Field-Grassy-Abner-Docs Ponds	South	4.4	50
Camp Cachalot	South	4.8	52
Frogfoot Brook	South	5.9	54
D. East			
East Entrance Hike 1	East	3.0	56
East Entrance Friends Hike	East	3.4	57
East Entrance Hike 3	East	4.7	58
Snake Hill Loop	East	4.5	60
Wing Holes from Alden Rd	East	6.3	62
Wing Holes/Saw Pit from Cutter Field Rd	East	3.9	64
E-Line Road from Mast Road	East	4.6	66

Ponds in MSSF

Pond Name	Size (acres)	Maximum Depth (feet)	Location in forest	Page
Three Cornered	14	4	Central	22
Torrey	3	4	Central	20
New Long	23	6	Central	11
Round	10	12	Central	22
College	53	24	Central	11
Bumps	20	4	East	-
Cherry	2	-	North-central	18
Hooper	3	-	North-central	-
Little College	3	-	North-central	-
Little Widgeon	7	5	Northwest	30
Widgeon	24	12	Northwest	-
Rocky	20	19	Northwest	34
Curlew	43	31	Northwest	32
Manters Hole	2	-	Northwest	32
Federal Pond	129		Northwest	36
Charge	23	17	South	48
Fearing	24	20	South	46
Doctors	2	3	Southeast	50
New Grassy	6	4	Southeast	50
Grassy	3	-	Southeast	50
East Head Reservoir	86	10	Southwest	26
Barrett	16	17	Southwest	42

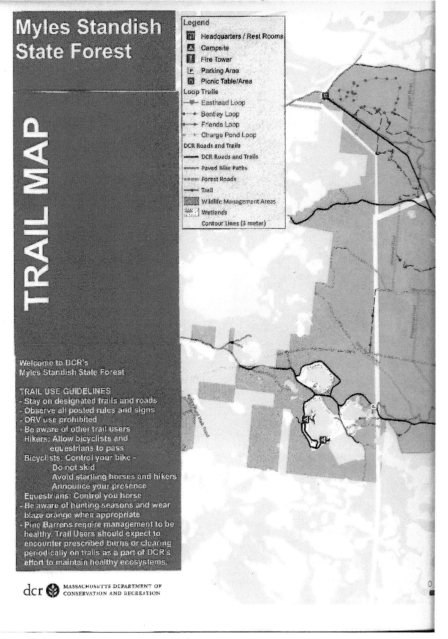

Myles Standish State Forest

TRAIL MAP

Legend

- 🏢 Headquarters / Rest Rooms
- ⛺ Campsite
- 🗼 Fire Tower
- 🅿 Parking Area
- 🍽 Picnic Table/Area

Loop Trails
- Easthead Loop
- Bentley Loop
- Friends Loop
- Charge Pond Loop

DCR Roads and Trails
- DCR Roads and Trails
- Paved Bike Paths
- Forest Roads
- Trail
- Wildlife Management Areas
- Wetlands
- Contour Lines (3 meter)

Welcome to DCR's
Myles Standish State Forest

TRAIL USE GUIDELINES
- Stay on designated trails and roads
- Observe all posted rules and signs
- ORV use prohibited
- Be aware of other trail users
  Hikers: Allow bicyclists and
          equestrians to pass
  Bicyclists: Control your bike -
          Do not skid
          Avoid startling horses and hikers
          Announce your presence
  Equestrians: Control you horse
- Be aware of hunting seasons and wear
  blaze orange when appropriate
- Pine Barrens require management to be
  healthy. Trail Users should expect to
  encounter prescribed burns or clearing
  periodically on trails as a part of DCR's
  effort to maintain healthy ecosystems.

dcr 🌳 MASSACHUSETTS DEPARTMENT OF
       CONSERVATION AND RECREATION

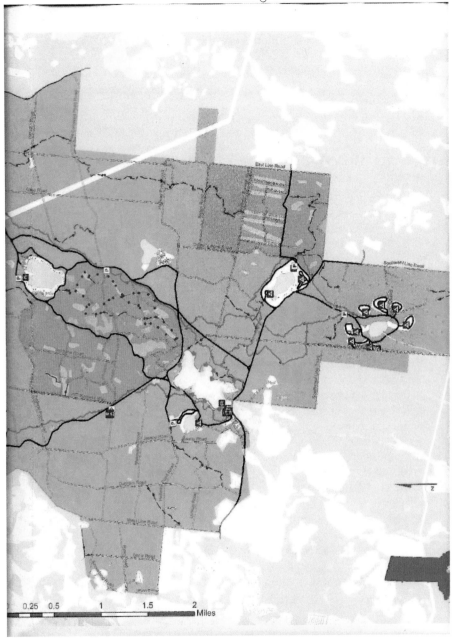

Significant Myles Standish State Forest Events

1500-1620 Area inhabited by Wampanoag Federation ("People of the First Light").

1616-1619 Plague reduced Wampanoag population to approximately 10% of its original size.

1620 English Puritans settle in Plymouth Harbor.

1675-1676 King Phillip's War devastated the remaining local Wampanoag population.

1710-1715 Ten Great Lots, including MSSF, granted by the Town of Plymouth to individuals, primarily for wood lots.

1770s Local fishing, whaling and shipbuilding industries required vast quantities of timber.

1793-1841 Federal Furnace of Carver used local fuel and bog iron to manufacture iron products.

1830 Original forest completely cut over.

1868 East Head Reservoir dammed to provide water source for cranberry production.

1880-1894 Job Turner operated farm for horses, cattle and poultry east of Barrett Pond.

1908 Massachusetts Game Sanctuary Association purchased 5,700 acres at MSSF.

1916 State Forest Commission acquires 5,700 acres in Carver and Plymouth creating Myles Standish State Forest.

1918 To raise revenue and secure the forest, the Forest Commission advertised the availability of 250 campsites for use around five ponds in the forest.

1930-1932 Department of Conservation hired unemployed men to construct new public campsites at Charge and Long ponds, plant 575,000 pine trees and construct 30 miles of roads.

1933-1937 CCC Camp S-56 constructed over 70 miles of roads, 17 miles of hiking trails, three cedar log bathhouses, several day use and camping areas and planted 730,000 pine trees.

1941-1945 War transportation restrictions and shortages reduced maintenance and attendance.

1951 New prison camp provides labor for park, road and timber management.

1957 Fire burns 12,500 acres, including 3,000 acres in the forest.

1964 Fire burns 1,500 acres in the forest, including recreation facilities at Charge Pond.

1970-1972 250 campsites, eight comfort stations, roads and utilities constructed at Charge Pond.

From: www.friendsmssf.com/rmp/rmp-mssf.pdf

The Hikes

The hikes are sorted into A. Central, B. West, C. South, and D. East areas, and then from north to south.

Directions assume you are coming from Rt. 3 and will enter via the East Entrance. If you are coming from the west on Cranberry Road. Follow it to the Forest Headquarters and then make a left on Lower College Pond Road. Most directions will include Lower or Upper College Pond Road. The map available at the headquarters will get you to the starting point.

A. Hikes in Central Area
Around College Pond

Directions and parking

From Rt. 3 Exit 5 go towards Long Pond Road. Go about two miles south on Long Pond Road to the entrance of MSSF. From Rt. 3, Exit 3 go about 3 miles north on Long Pond Road to the entrance of MSSF. Enter the park. Go about 1 ¾ miles to the first intersection. Turn left onto Upper College Pond Road. Go about 1 mile to the parking lot (P2 on park map) on the right by Three Cornered Pond Road.
Approximate GPS address Upper College Pond Rd., Plymouth, MA

Features

Small ponds, College Pond, tree lined dirt roads, wooded trails. College Pond[4] is a 53-acre (210,000 m^2) natural kettle hole pond in Plymouth, Massachusetts, located in the Myles Standish State Forest northeast of East Head Reservoir, Three Cornered Pond, New Long Pond and Barrett Pond, and north of Fearing Pond. There is a swimming beach and picnic area along the north shore of the pond.

Difficulty

5.1 miles; 2 hrs; no difficult terrain.
4.5 miles , 1:45 hrs., no difficult terrain

Hike 1 5.1 miles green trail on map

Start the hike in the northeast corner of the lot. Cross Three Cornered Pond Rd. The trail starts a few feet west of Upper College Pond Road. Head northwest following the the blue markers. When you come to the open field stay right and then turn left near the end of the field. Again follow the blue markers. At the T s stay right. The trail will turn northwest again. After you turn right at the second intersection the trail will no longer be marked. At the next intersectioon make a sharp left and work your way around the small pond till you get to Lower College Pond Road. There is an opening to the right to go between two small ponds. The one on the left being Torrey Pond. At Lower College Pond Road make a right and follow the road a little less than ½ mile. Find the dirt road on the left, which eventually turns into Wayout Roasd.. Follow Wayout Road north to Howland Road. Follow Howland Road to Snake Hill Road. Turn right and stay right till you see Cranford Road on the left. There will be "cottages" visible along College Pond from this road. When Cranford Road turns west, stay left and come out on Upper College Pond Road. The parking lot is a few feet south.

Hike 2 4.5 miles red shortcuts on map

Start the hike in the northeast corner of the lot. Cross Three Cornered Pond Rd. The trail starts a few feet west of Upper College Pond Road. Head northwest following the blue markers. When you come to the open field stay right and then turn right near the end of the field. At the next junction turn left and then left again onto West Cranford Road. Follow it to Lower College Pond Road. Cross the street go the right look for Fderal Furnace Road on the left. Take Federal Furnace Road ~500 ft to the trail on the right. Follow it north and north east till it emerges on Howland Road. Turn right and follow Howland Road to Snake Hill Road. Turn right and stay right till you see Cranford Road on the left. There will be "cottages" visible along College Pond from this road. When Cranford Road turns west, stay left and come out on Upper College Pond Road. The parking lot is a few feet south.

Ponds along the trail

Frank Werny

Trails around College Pond

Bentley Loop
Directions and parking
From Rt. 3 Exit 5 go towards Long Pond Road. Go about two miles south on Long Pond Road to the entrance of MSSF.
From Rt. 3, Exit 3 go about 3 miles north on Long Pond Road to the entrance of MSSF.
Enter the park. Go about 1 ¾ miles to the first intersection. Turn left onto Upper College Pond Road. Go about 1 mile to the parking lot (P2 on park map) on the right by Three Cornered Pond Road.
Approximate GPS address Upper College Pond Rd and Three Cornered Pond Road., Plymouth, MA

Features
Bob Bentley, a longtime member of the Carver Conservation Commission and a legend in local conservation circles, laid out the Bentley Loop trail and has worked to maintain it for the last 30 years.
The trail goes through the woods, it comes close to Three Cornered Pond, New Long Pond and Round Pond and passes by several large meadows.

Difficulty
3.7 miles, 2 hours, some short steep ups and downs.

Hike
Start the hike from the marked northwest corner of the parking lot. This is a very well-marked trail. There are both 'Bentley Loop 'signs and blue markings on trees. Follow the blue marks on the trees. At any double mark a change in direction is required. If you see a double blue mark, look for the next single mark and follow it. From the beginning the trail heads southwest and then down the middle of a meadow. Just past the meadow it turns south. Keep following the blue marks. After about ½ mile it will turn right, and after another ½ mile it will make a very sharp right and head northeast. Follow it past the spot where you can see an unnamed pond. Turn right onto Negus Road and then search for blue marks on the left. The trail will now take you past, but not to, Three Cornered Pond and Round Pond. Make a right and then a left after Round Pond. At the meadow stay to your left and exit left. Now follow the trail southeast through the woods and past another meadow. A sharp left at the end of the meadow will take you back to the parking lot.

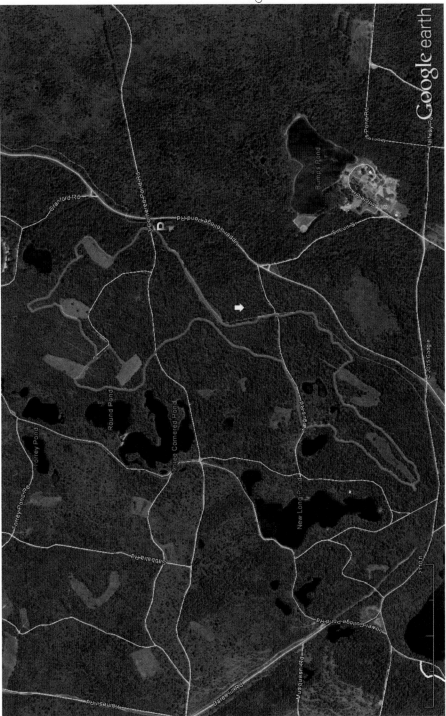

Bentley Loop Trail

15

Central MSSF and Fire Tower Hike

Directions

From Rt. 3, Exit 3 go Right on CLARK RD. Turn Right on Long Pond Rd - go 2.0 mi. Turn Left on Alden Rd - go 1.4 mi. Continue on Lower College Pond Rd – about 2 1/4 miles, turn right onto Bare Hill Road, go about ½ mile, then turn left at the corner of Bare Hill and Three Cornered Pond Roads into the parking lot by the fire tower and park there.

Approximate GPS: Bare Hill Road & Three Cornered Pond Rd, Plymouth, MA

Features

This is a quiet hike on dirt roads in the Forest. All woods, no bogs or ponds. Use a map obtainable at Forest Headquarters

Difficulty

4.2 miles; mostly flat; about 1:30 hours

Hike

From the parking lot, cross Bare Hill Road and turn left onto Kamesit Way. This is a straight dirt road heading north along a gas line easement. Go past Torrey Pond Rd, then Federal Pond Road, and turn right on Pokanoket Road. Go about ¾ mile east, then turn right onto Wayout Road. Follow it about ½ mile and then turn right on Federal Pond Road. After less than ½ mile turn left onto Sabbiatia Road. When it dead ends on Three Cornered Pond Road turn right and continue west to the fire tower and the parking lot.

Wintery Kamesit Way

Fire Tower

Fire Tower Trail

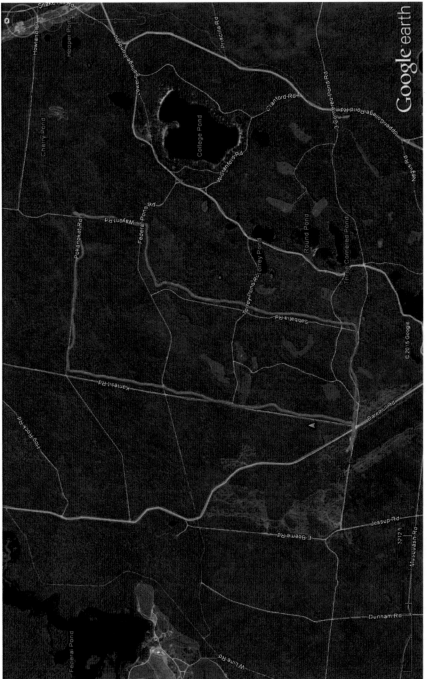

Cherry Pond Valley

Directions

From Rt. 3 Exit 5 go towards Long Pond Road. Go about two miles south on Long Pond Road to the entrance of MSSF.

From Rt. 3, Exit 3 go about 3 miles north on Long Pond Road to the entrance of MSSF.

Enter the park. Go about 1 ¾ miles to the first intersection. Continue straight on Lower College Pond Road. Go almost 1.4 miles to Federal Furnace Road on the right. Park here without blocking the road.

Features

Cherry Pond is a 2 acre lake and is located in MSSF, Plymouth County, Massachusetts, United States. The elevation above sea level is 32 meters. It's a scenic spot and well worth the short hike.

Difficulty

2.8 miles; 2 hours moving time, some hills

Hike

From the intersection walk up Federal Furnace Road. After about 250 feet there will be a trail on the right. Follow the trail north till it makes a sharp turn to the right after about ½ mile. Turn right. You will see two steep trails going down to Cherry Pond. Pass them up. Continue on the trail as it turns north and get to Howland Road., a small, straight dirt road. Turn left. At the bottom of the next hill look for a trail to the left. It will take you to Cherry Pond. Go to the right with the pond on the left and then take a trail west down the center of Cherry Pond Valley. Continue west. There will be motor bike trails coming in and out, and at times the trail is almost nonexistent. But it is a beautiful valley and will take you to across Wayout Road, and then follow the valley southwest and up to a small dirt road, Pokanoket Road. Turn left on it and then right on Wayout Road. This will take you to Federal Furnace Road. Turn left again and follow the road back to the cars. You can also make a right turn after the road turns and just before it straightens out and bushwhack a few feet to the right into the logged area and then follow the open space southeast till you can see an un-named pond on the right and then continue down to Lower College Pond Road and turn left to get back to the parking area.

Cherry Pond   Cherry Pond Valley

Cherry Pond Valley Trail

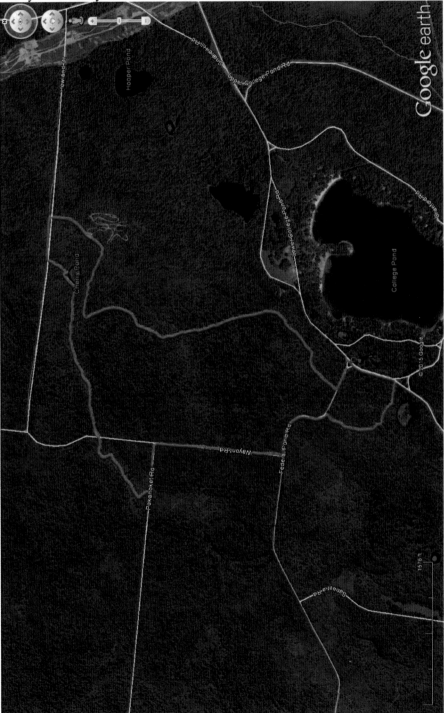

19

Fire Tower to Torrey Pond Loop

Directions
From Rt. 3, Exit 3 go Right on Clark Rd. Turn Right on Long Pond
Road - go 2.0 mi. Turn Left on Alden Road - go 1.4 mi. Continue on
Lower College Pond Road – about 2 miles, turn right onto Bare Hill
Road, go about ½ mile, then turn left at the corner of Bare Hill and
Three Cornered Pond Roads and then right into the parking lot by the
fire tower and park there.
GPS directions not available. Bare Hill Road, Plymouth, MA

Features
A quiet hike on dirt roads and trail in the woods. Torrey Pond 3 acres and 4 ft. deep.

Difficulty
3 miles. No significant hills.

Hike
Exit the parking lot cross Bare Hill Road. After about 500 feet take the dirt road
going left. Stay on it till after you cross Sabbatia Road. Then go about 500 feet and
turn left at the end of the open area. Cross the field staying right and take the trail in
the right hand corner of the field going north. Follow the trail north. At the junction
when you can see a water hole straight ahead, turn right. A secondary water hole
should be visible in front of you at first and then to your left. Follow the trail around
the east end of Torrey Pond to Torrey Pond Road. Just after you reach the road you
can make your way to the water on the left. Now follow the road west and across
Sabbatia Road. Once you cross Sabbatia look for a dirt road on the left. Turn left
onto the road and follow it. Just after the road makes a left turn there is a trail on the
right. It will take you to another dirt road, Kamesit Road. Turn left an after less than
a quarter mile arrive at the junction of Kamesit, Bare Hill, and d Three Cornered
pond Road. The parking area will be across the street.

Unnamed Hole

Torrey Pond

Torrey Pond

Meadows

Fire Tower Torrey Pond Loop Trail

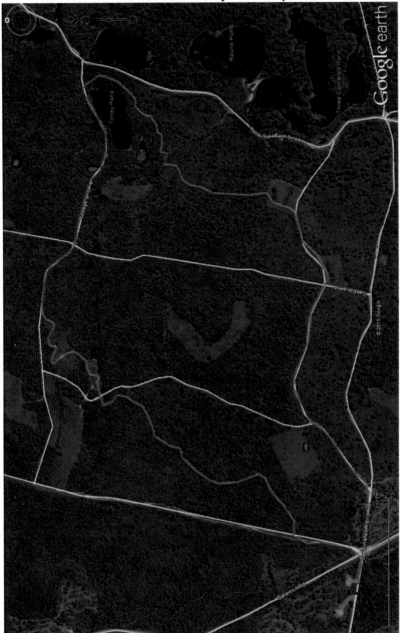

Three Cornered Pond

Directions and parking
From Rt. 3 Exit 5 go towards Long Pond Road. Go about two miles south on Long Pond Road to the entrance of MSSF.
From Rt. 3, Exit 3 go about 3 miles north on Long Pond Road to the entrance of MSSF..
Enter the park. Go about 1 ¾ miles to the first intersection. Turn left onto Upper College Pond Road. Go about 1 mile to the parking lot (P2 on park map) on the right. Approximate GPS address: Upper College Pond Rd., Plymouth, MA

Hike Difficulty
4.1 miles, 1:40 hrs. Some hills.

Features
New Long Pond, Three Cornered Pond, Round Pond, ponds, and pines.
New Long Pond[4] is a 23-acre pond in MSSF located northeast of East Head Reservoir and southwest of College Pond and Three-Cornered Pond. The water quality is impaired due to non-native aquatic plants.
Three Cornered Pond[4] is a 14-acre pond in MSSF located northeast of New Long Pond and southwest of College Pond. The water quality is also impaired due to non-native aquatic plants.

The Hike
Secure a park map at headquarters. The trail starts in the southwest corner of the parking lot and goes south from there parallel to the road. After crossing Negus Rd it will be on the bike path. When you get to Halfway Pond Road, make a right. Follow the road for about ¼ mile and look for the trail on the right. Follow the trail to a dirt road, Negus Rd, turn right. Go about ¼ miles. Look for the trail markers on the left. Take the trail across Three Cornered Pond Road to a corner of Three-Cornered Pond. Bear right, go past Round Pond. After the pond, about ¼ mile, make a sharp right; then a sharp left following the trail markers. At the open field stay to your left and make a left down the hill again following the trail markers. Past the bottom of the hill the trail make a sharp right. Going straight would take you to College Pond. Follow the trail to the open field entering on the north corner. Follow the field around on the left and then find the trail at the south corner of the field. The trail will take you back to the parking lot.

New Long Pond   Three Cornered Pond

Three Cornered Pond Hike

East Head Reservoir from Forest Headquarters
Directions and parking
From Rt.3 Exit 5 take Long Pond Road south to MSSF East Entrance. From Exit 3 take Long Pond Road north. After entering MSSF, follow signs to Headquarters, ~five miles. Park in Headquarters lower parking lot.
Approximate GPS address: 257 Cranberry Rd, Carver, MA 02330, USA

Hike Difficulty
2.6 miles; 1:10 hours, flat, some short hills, marked trail

Features
Forest trail; Easthead Reservoir; nature trail; Forest Headquarters East Head Reservoir; beautiful pond, marked nature spots (brochure available at park headquarters).
East Head Reservoir[4], is a 92-acre pond with a maximum depth of 10 feet. The reservoir is the headwaters to the Wankinco River and a water supply for private bogs southwest of the headquarters.

The Hike
From the middle of the parking lot, take a trail to the left or northeast. Follow it to a small peninsula. Then turn around and go to your right. The trail will follow the shore of the pond. Follow the blue triangle markers, which however go the other way. After about 3/4 mile the trail leaves the pond shore and approaches the road. Take the crosswalk and continue on the trail across the street. (Red line on map) It will emerge at another cross walk, putting you back on the trail along the shore. Near the western corner of the pond, the trail emerges on a gas line trail. Follow the gas lines to the right and after about 100 feet, there is a continuation of the trail to the right. Follow the trail mostly along the shoreline again to the southern point of the pond. Here the trail cuts over to the end of Fearing Pond Road. After crossing the reservoir dam, you will be back at the parking lot.

Flow Control

View of Reservoir

East Head Reservoir Trail

Easthead Reservoir from P2
Directions and parking
From Rt. 3 Exit 5 go towards Long Pond Road. Go about two miles south on Long Pond Road to the entrance of MSSF.
From Rt. 3, Exit 3 go about 3 miles north on Long Pond Road to the entrance of MSWSF
Enter the park. Go about 1 ¾ miles to the first intersection. Turn left onto Upper College Pond Road. Go about 1 mile to the parking lot (P2 on park map) on the right by Three Cornered Pond Road.
Approximate GPS address Upper College Pond Rd., Plymouth, MA

Features
Forest trail; Easthead Reservoir; nature trail; Forest Headquarters, see previous hike

Difficulty
5.2 miles; 2:15 hours; some moderately steep ups and downs from the parking lot to the reservoir; mostly flat around the reservoir.

Water Control

Overgrown area

Hike
Start the hike in the northwest corner of the parking lot, just to the left of the northern bulletin board. In general start out following the blue trail markers heading south west. Go right down the middle of the first meadow. Past the end make a slight left and turn south. After you cross Negus Road, dirt road, turn southwest again till you get to the next meadow. There take the trail to the right and into the woods. Follow it southwest till you get to the tip of a meadow and several intersecting trail. Continue straight to the dirt road and turn left. This will take you out to Halfway Pond Road. Cross and find a small trail to the left of the telephone pole. Follow it to the clearing for the gas lines. Turn right and search for a trail to the left towards the reservoir. If you get to the road you went too far. Follow the trail around the reservoir clockwise. Near the park headquarters the trail emerges on a road and you need to cross the reservoir dam on the road. At this point you may visit the headquarters or continue following the trail clockwise around the reservoir again. At some point the trail emerges on the road again, but shortly continues on around the reservoir on a nice trail. This portion has several boardwalk sections. When you get to the gas line clearings turn right and look for the small trail on the left that will take you back to Halfway Pond Road. You can also turn left and then right on Halfway Pond Road. At the telephone pole with the trail cross and retrace your steps back to the car.

Easthead Reservoir from Parking Lot 2

B. Western Area

Northwest Corner

Directions
From Rt. 3 Exit 3 got to Long Pond Road. Turn right, go 2 miles. Turn left at the MSSF entrance onto Alden Road. After almost 2 miles go straight at the intersection onto Lower College Pond Road. Go about 2.5 miles and turn right unto Bare Hill Roads. Go about 3 miles north to Curlew Pond Road on the left. Park before the gate if it is closed. If open proceed to the paved parking area on right.
Approximate GPS address: 1 Curlew Pond Road, Plymouth, MSA 02360

Features
Just forest trails. Some motor bike tracks.

Difficulty
3.8 miles, sandy trails, some steep hills.

Hike
If you parked outside the gate, walk on the road to the paved parking lot on the right. The trail starts in the back right corner. After the trail turns left continue straight/northwest crossing some sandy trails. After you come down the 2nd hill there will be a wet hole on the left. Continue to stay left and continue on the trail till it makes a sharp left turn. To the left will be Manters Hole. Turn right and follow this trail north for about 1 mile. When the trail gets to some sandy cross trails make a sharp right and then another sharp right. Bypass the sandy trail to the right and continue meandering and then the trail turns south and joins another trail coming in from the left. Follow the trail south for about a mile, going through 2 sandy bike track areas. At the 3rd sandy area stay left and come back to the trail you started on and turn left. To get there you will have to cross several trees that have been placed in your way to stop motor-bike traffic. This trail will take you back to the paved parking area.

Along the trail

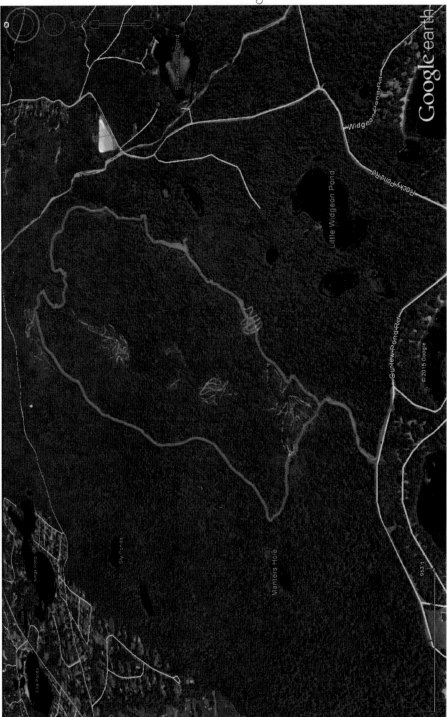

NW Corner Trail

Little Widgeon Pond

Directions
From Exit 3 Rte. 3 got west to Long Pond Road. Turn right, go 2 miles. Turn left at the Myles Standish State Park entrance onto Alden Road. After about 2 miles continue straight onto Lower College Pond Rd. After about 2 mi turn sharp right onto Bare Hill Rd. Go 3.0 mi. Continue as it turns into Rocky Pond Rd. When you get to the power lines crossing the road, just before the solar farm, park on the left by the gate to the power lines.
Approximate GPS address: 290 Rocky Pond Rd, Plymouth, MA 02360.

Features
Little Widgeon Pond, a 7 acre pond with a maximum depth of 5 feet. Quiet forest trails.

Difficulty
2.5 miles, some steep hills.

Hike
From the power lines walk back/south along Rocky Point Road till you get to a gate on the right. Go around it and walk on a wide dirt road. Stay left and follow the road down to Little Widgeon Pond. Up from the pond and to the left are a few remnants of an old camp. Turn back on the road you came on and go almost to the gate, but turn left on a trail leading downhill, by a small pond and then over to another valley. Turn right and follow the valley northeast for almost ½ mile and then take a steep trail to the right. This will take you to the power lines and the parking area on the right.

Little Widgeon Pond

Camp remnant   Small pond

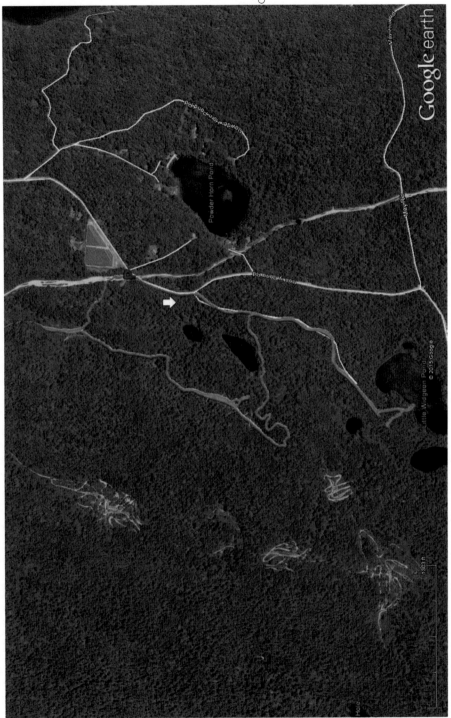

Little Widgeon Pond Trail

Curlew Pond Loop

Directions
From Rt. 3 Exit 3 got to Long Pond Road. Turn right, go 2 miles. Turn left at the MSSF entrance onto Alden Road. After almost 2 miles go straight at the intersection onto Lower College Pond Road. Go about 2.5 miles and turn right unto Bare Hill Roads. Go about 3 miles north to Curlew Pond Road on the left. Park before the gate if it is closed. If open proceed to the paved parking area on right.
Approximate GPS address: 1 Curlew Pond Road, Plymouth, MSA 02360

Features
Curlew Pond 43 acres 31 feet deep. Manters Hole 2 acres, Curlew Pond Campground

Difficulty
3 miles, some short steep hills, mostly in the woods.

Hike
If you parked outside the gate, walk on the road to the paved parking lot on the right. The trail starts in the back right corner. After the trail turns left continue straight/northwest crossing some sandy trails. After you come down the 2nd hill there will be a wet hole on the left. Continue to stay left and continue on the trail till it makes a sharp left turn. You are now parallel to Manters Hole. In the winter you can see it on the right. Should you want to go to the water level of Manters Hole cross over about 100 feet west to another trail. Along this trail look for a convenient way to fight your way down to the water. There are no trails around the hole. Make your way back up the trail and turn right or south, or cross over to the one you came on and go right also. The trails will merge after less than ¼ mile. Continue on the merged trail as it turns south. When you see a water hole on the right turn left and pass with the water on your right. The trail will take you east to Rocky Pond Road, a dirt road in the woods. Turn left and pass between Rocky Pond and Curlew on this road. You will see evidence of a trailer park on the Curlew Pond side and a bog on the right. Turn left by the sandy area across from Rocky Pond and then turn right onto a trail to S. Curlew Pond Road. This will take you out to the now paved Rocky Pond Road. Turn left, go a few steps and turn left onto Curlew Pond Road. Follow it back to the parking area.

Manters Hole

Curlew Pond

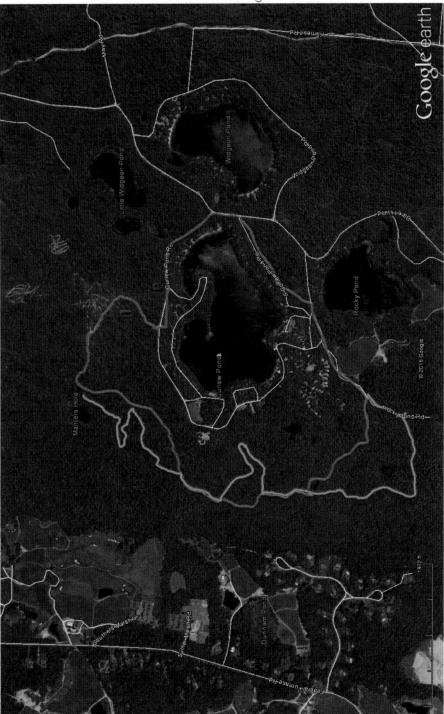

Curlew Loop Trail. Red as described. Green are additional trails.

Federal and Rocky Ponds

Directions

From Rt. 3 Exit 3 go west on Clark Road to Long Pond Road. Turn right and go about 2 miles to MSSF Entrance. This is Alden Road.
It turns into Lower College Pond Road. After about 4 miles from the entrance, make a right onto Bare Hill Road. After about 1 ½ miles you come to Federal Pond Road. Just beyond Federal Pond Road on the left, there is an area suitable for parking.
Approximate GPS: Federal Pond & Bare Hill Road

Features

Federal Cranberry Bogs, Federal and Rocky ponds, pines,
Federal Pond is a 129-acre (0.52 km^2) pond in Carver and Plymouth, Massachusetts. A small portion of the northeastern shore of the pond is in the Myles Standish State Forest. The pond is located southwest of Rocky and Curlew Ponds, and northeast of Dunham Pond. Two unnamed islands lie in the middle of the pond. The water quality is impaired due to non-native aquatic plants and non-native fish species.
The only road leading to the pond, Old Federal Road in Carver, is a private road. As such, the pond is officially off limits to the public, although a high-tension line right of way crosses the northern tip of the pond and is frequented by sport fishermen.
Rocky Pond is an 18-acre (73,000 m^2) pond in the MSSF. The pond is located south of Curlew Pond.

Difficulty

5.2 miles; 2 hrs. Some short hills.

Hike

From the parking area, walk back to Federal Pond Road, and turn right/west. Follow the sandy road till you get to another dirt road, West Line Rd. Here turn left and shortly again right. Walk down and take in the view of the large bog area, Federal Bogs, and the farmhouse across the bogs. Beyond here, everything is private. So, turn around go back to West Line Road and turn left. Follow West Line Road for a little over a mile. Then take a smaller trail to the left. It will take you to the power lines and the northeast tip of Federal Pond. A few feet east along the power lines, a trail goes off to the left. Follow it in the woods in the direction of the power lines. After a little more than ¼ mile take a trail going northwest away from the power lines. It will bump into Rocky Pond Rd. Turn right and follow Rocky Pond Rd till you get to a bog area on the right. Follow the road to the end of the bog than turn right and follow the edge of the bog. Make a sharp right and continue to follow the bog till you see Rocky Pond on the left and another bog area on the right. Follow the edge of the bog to its south corner and then take a path up to and across the power lines, up to Bare Hill Rd. Go south on Bare Hill Rd. Look for the bicycle trail on the left. Cross over to it when you can and follow it to Federal Pond Rd, turn right, go to Bare Hill Rd and make another right and the car will be just on the left.

Federal Pond   Rocky Pond

Federal & Rocky Ponds Trail

Around Federal Pond

Another option is to hike around Federal Pond, but the trail does pass to the side of some privately owned bogs.

Directions
From Rt. 3 Exit 3 turn west on Clark Road. At Long Pond Road turn right, go 2 miles. Turn left at the MSSF road onto Alden Road. After almost 2 miles go straight at the intersection onto Lower College Pond Road. Go about 2.5 miles and turn right unto Bare Hill Roads. Go about 3 miles north to the Rocky Pond parking lot on the left. Approximate GPS directions: About ½ mile south of 149 Bare Hill Rd, Plymouth MA in MSSF.

Features
MSSF, Federal Pond, Rocky Pond, Federal Bogs (private)
Federal Pond is a 129-acre (0.52 km^2) pond in Carver and Plymouth, Massachusetts. A small portion of the northeastern shore of the pond is in MSSF. Two unnamed islands lie in the middle of the pond.
The only road leading to the pond, Old Federal Road in Carver, is a private road. As such, the pond is officially off limits to the public, although a high tension line right of way crosses the northern tip of the pond and is frequented by sport fishermen.
For comparison: Billington Sea is 269 acres and Herring Pond is 376 acres.

Difficulty
4.8 miles, some short hills and 150 feet of bushwhacking.

Hike
From the northwest corner of the parking lot go downhill and then pass around the small bog, with the bog on your right. At the northwestern tip of the bog turn left and then left again. Cross the power lines and go to Federal Pond. There turn right and follow the pond on your left. Go under the power lines once and the second time follow them west. There will be two trails on the left taking you to spits of land. Come back up to the power lines. Continue west or to the left to the next trail on the left. Take it to the pond and then follow the trail around the pond, with the pond on your left. Continue with the pond on your left on Old Federal Road (private) and eventually pass some bogs on your right. Follow the contours of the pond on your left. You will pass through an area with buildings. This is private property. We have not had a problem walking through and continuing on the left towards the bog directly by the pond. Here go to the right hand or southeast corner, climb up a short hill, turn slightly to your right and bushwhack to West Line Road, the border of the state forest. Turn left and follow the road for about a mile. Do not turn left. You will emerge on Bare Hill Road, turn left and find the car about 1000 ft. up the road.

Rocky Pond

Federal Pond

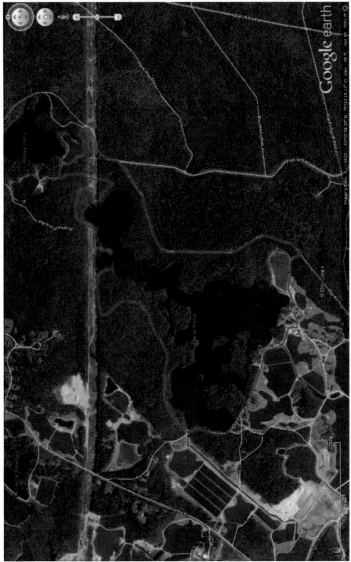

Trail around Federal Pond

Lost Horse Bog

Directions and parking
From Rt. 3 Exit 5 go towards Long Pond Road. Go about two miles south on Long Pond Road to the entrance of MSSF.

From Rt. 3, Exit 3 go about 3 miles north on Long Pond Road to the entrance of MSSF.

Enter the park. Go about 1 ¾ miles to the first intersection. Continue straight on Lower College Pond Road. Go almost 3 miles then make a right onto Halfway Pond Road. There is a sign pointing to the equestrian parking lot (P3 on the Forest map). Follow the signs to Equestrian Parking Lot (P3) at Jessup Rd and Halfway Pond Rd. GPS: Jessup & Halfway Pond Roads.

Features
Quiet dirt roads through the woods leading to a quiet isolated bog. Lost Horse Bog. http://www.wickedlocal.com/plymouth/news/x1985977218/Little-known-area-of-Myles-Standish-State-Forest-catches-attention-of-the-state

Difficulty
5.2 miles on flat dirt roads, some gradual uphill and downhill; narrow trail around the bog. About 2 hrs.

Hike
From the parking lot go back out to HALFWAY Pond Road and turn left/west. Continue due west. Cross Dunham, Road, and then West Line Road. Continue to Shaw Road. (All about ½ mile apart, all are marked with red forest signs.) Make a right onto Shaw Road, then turn left onto Ryan Road. Near the end of Ryan Road, before you get to the houses, make a left onto a smaller road going southeast, which leads to the bog. You may hike around the bog and retrace your steps back to the car. Or, from the east corner of the bog bushwhack east out to Shaw Road. Turn right and make your way back to Halfway Pond Road. Turn left and make your way back to the car.

Lost Horse Bog   Bog and Water Supply

Lost Horse Bog from Equestrian parking Lot, P3

Shady Acres Campground (W)

Directions
From Rt. 3 Exit 5 go towards Long Pond Road. Go about two miles south on Long Pond Road to the entrance of MSSF.
From Rt. 3, Exit 3 go about 3 miles north on Long Pond Road to the entrance of MSSF. Enter the park. Go about 1 ¾ miles to the first intersection. Continue straight on Lower College Pond Road. Go almost 3 miles then make a right onto Bare Hill Road. After ~1 mile make a left onto Three Cornered Pond Road and park in the parking lot on the right, P6.
Approximate GPS address: Three cornered Pond Road and Bare Hill Road, Plymouth, MA

Features
Shady Acres Camp Ground, http://www.shadyacrescamping.com
Lost Horse Bog, bogs, forest pond.

Difficulty
6.5 miles, mostly flat, mostly wide sandy dirt roads.

Hike
From the parking lot go to Three Cornered Pond Road and turn right. Follow it for almost 1 mile to a T. Turn right, then take your first left onto Shoestring Road. Pass a small bog on the right and then after ½ mile take a right. Now continue around the bog, with the bog on your left. After the bog make a right and follow the water on your left. At the road turn left and walk past the sandy area into the Shady Acres Campground. In the summer this a good place to buy some refreshments for the way back. From the office area zigzag your way to the east side of the camp and take Ryan Road east. After about 100 feet turn right and walk down to Lost Horse Bog, circle it and come back to Ryan Road. Turn right and continue about ½ mile to the T. Turn left and then take your first right onto 3 Cornered Pond Road. This will take you back to the parking lot on the left.

Bogs

Shady Acres

Lost Horse Bog

Shady Acres Hike

Barrett Pond

Directions
From Rt. 3 Exit 5 go towards Long Pond Road. Go about two miles south on Long Pond Road to the entrance of MSSF.

From Rt. 3, Exit 3 go about 3 miles north on Long Pond Road to the entrance of MSSF.

Enter the park. Go about 1 ¾ miles to the first intersection. Continue straight on Lower College Pond Road. Go almost 3 miles then make a right onto Halfway Pond Road. There is a sign pointing to the equestrian parking lot (P3 on the Forest map). Follow the signs to Equestrian Parking Lot (P3) at Jessup Rd and Halfway Pond Rd. GPS: Jessup & Halfway Pond Roads.

Features
Barrett Pond, Bogs, quiet forest trails

Difficulty
3 miles, some hills.

Hike
From the northwest corner of the lot take the trail that parallels the road at first, but about 100 feet after crossing Jessup Road turns away from the road going southwest. Follow it till you get to a dirt road (Lunxus Rd). Turn left and find a trail on the right after about 100 feet. Continue to the next road (Dunham Road) and turn left. At Cranberry Road turn left again. Pass the house and bog on the left and then turn left at the east end of the property. Follow the eastern edge and then continue on the trail. At the next bog stay left and proceed to your left on Jessup Road. When you reach the next road on your right with a sign indicating a 'drafting' area turn right and go straight down to Barrett Pond. Once at Barrett Pond take the narrow trail to the left a few feet from the water. Follow the trail with the pond on the right till you come to the raised platform. Continue on to the paved road and then after about 200 feet make a left onto another paved road and go straight back to the parking lot.

Deer skeleton in the bog reservoir   Barrett Pond

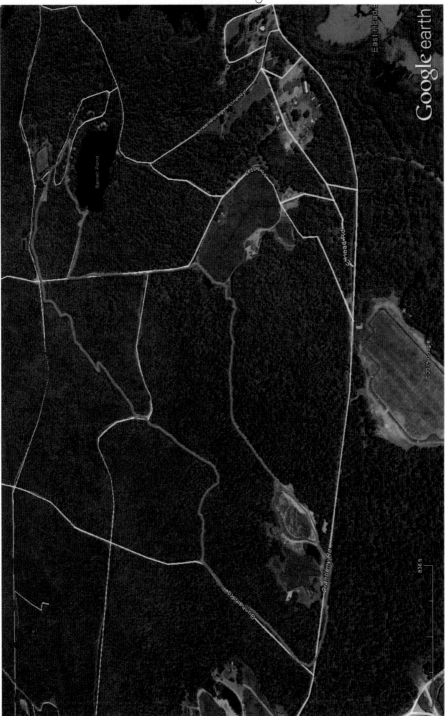

Barrett Pond Loop

Equestrian Lot/Grady Pond Loop

Directions

From Rt. 3 Exit 5 go towards Long Pond Road. Go about two miles south on Long Pond Road to the entrance of MSSF.

From Rt. 3, Exit 3 turn west on Clark Rd. Turn right onto Long Pond Road and go about 3 miles north on Long Pond Road to the entrance of MSSF.

Enter the park. Go about 1 ¾ miles to the first intersection. Continue straight on Lower College Pond Road. Go almost 3 miles then make a right onto Halfway Pond Road. There is a sign pointing to the equestrian parking lot (P3 on the Forest map). Follow the signs to Equestrian Parking Lot (P3) at Jessup Rd and Halfway Pond Rd. GPS: Jessup & Halfway Pond Roads.

Features
Quiet walk on wide dirt roads and trails in the woods. Grady Pond.

Difficulty
2.8 miles, some hills.

Hike
From the northwest corner of the lot take the trail that parallels the road at first. After crossing Jessup go up to Halfway Pond Road and continue west on it. After crossing Dunham Road. The first dirt road will take you down to a small water hole if you are interested. Return and turn left. After about 200 feet take the trail to the left which will bring you out on W Line Road in the Grady Pond area. Turn left, pass Grady Pond on the right, and then make a left onto Lunxus Road. Follow it, cross over Dunham Road and then when the road turns left and then sharp right look for a trail on your left. It will take you back to Halfway Pond Road. Turn right and make your way back to the parking area.

Dunham Road

Grady Pond

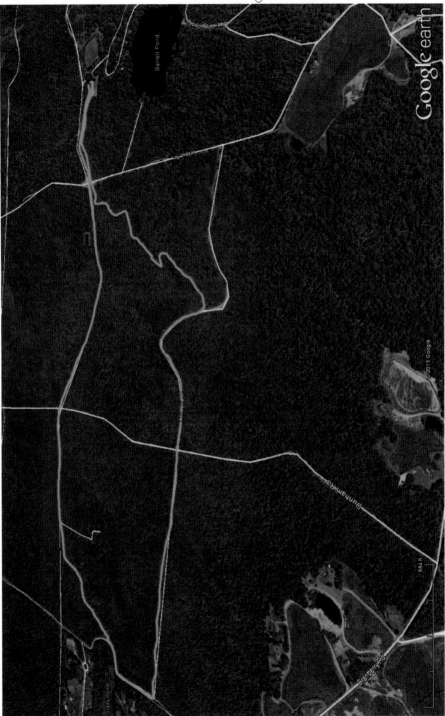

C. Southern Area

Charge and Fearing Pond Area

Directions and parking

From Rt. 3, Exit 3 turn west on Clark Rd. Turn right onto Long Pond Road and go about 3 miles north on Long Pond Road to the entrance of MSSF Go about 1 ¾ miles to the first intersection. Turn left onto Upper College Pond Road. Go about 3 miles and turn left on Fearing Pond Road. Then turn left onto Charge Pond Road. There will be a parking area on the right about ½ mile west on Charge Pond Road. In the winter Charge Pond Road is closed and you will have to park off road by the gate and walk in.

Approximate GPS address: 400 Charge Pond Rd., Plymouth, MA

Features

Fearing Pond, Charge Pond, Grassy Pond, campgrounds, Old Stone fireplaces.
Charge Pond[4] is a 23-acre warm water pond with an average depth of six feet and a maximum depth of 17 feet. The pond is fed by groundwater and is the headwaters to Harlow Brook.

Fearing Pond is a 24-acre (97,000 m^2) natural kettle hole pond with an average depth of ten feet and the maximum depth is 20 feet (6.1 m). Camp Squanto is nearby. The pond is fed by groundwater.

There are two hikes in this area. One about 3.5 miles and the other just over 5 miles.

Hike 1: Circles Charge and Fearing Ponds and is 3.5 miles
Hike 2: It makes a wide circle around Charge Pond

Hike 1

About 4.7 miles. 1:45 hours, not difficult. Some short hills around the ponds.

The Hike (Red Line)

From the parking lot, take the paved bicycle trail northwest. It will cross Southwest Line Rd and then Fearing Pond Road. Turn right, cross Circuit Road. After ~1/4 miles, you can leave the trail to the right and explore Fearing Pond. After you come back up to the road, turn right. Find the bike trail at the next street intersection (Doctors Pond Road) and follow it to the right. It will take you past Grassy Pond on the left. Continue to follow the bike trail south. It will pass a short cut to the parking lot. Continue till it ends in the campground off Charge Pond. Go down to Charge Pond. Now you can meander around Charge Pond, first along the shore, then along the road ending up on Charge Pond Road. You will find the parking lot ~ ¼ miles north up that road.

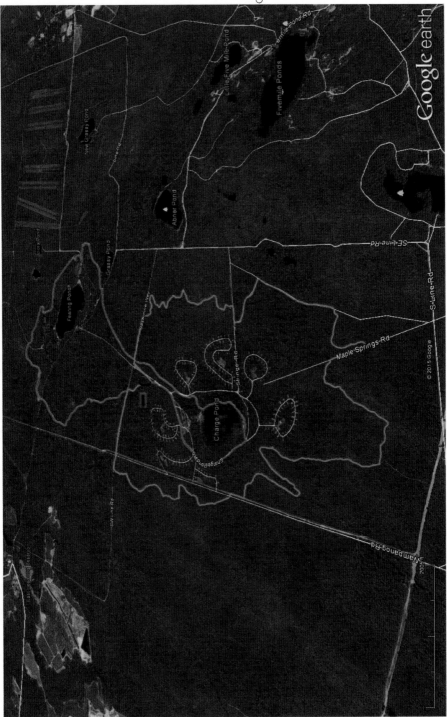

Charge and Fearing Ponds Trails

Hike 2 Charge Pond Loop
About 5.2 miles, mostly flat.

The Hike (green line)
Take the bike trail north from the northwest corner of the parking lot. When you reach Sasemine Way turn left. Go straight, cross Haynes Rd and then look for a trail with blue blazes on the left. Follow it south, spotting occasional blue blazes .When you emerge on Haynes Rd cross over and then go right about 100 yds. Take the trail on your left. There are red blazes. When you reach the water ditch turn right, go till you reach way across the water. Now go north and follow the trail. It will turn south again for ~1/2 mile. At the split stay left and follow the trail to Maple Spring Rd. Turn right on the dirt road till you find a trail on the left after about 500 ft. Follow the trail till you can clearly see a dirt road on your right. Bushwhack over onto an un-named dirt road. Turn left. After ~1/2 mile take the trail on the left over to Stringer Road. On Stringer Road turn right. After ~500 feet take the trail on the left. It meanders north about ½ mile. To Sasemine Road. There turn left. Continue to Charge Pond Road Turn left again and walk up to the parking area.

Old stone fire place   Charge Pond

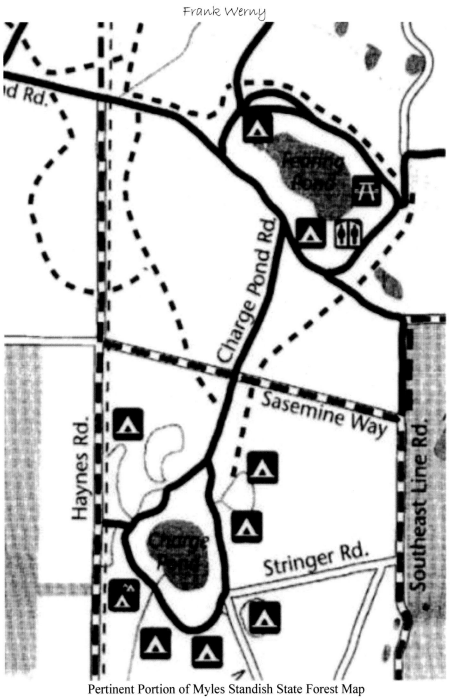

Pertinent Portion of Myles Standish State Forest Map

Hike Myles Standish State Forest
Four Small Ponds off Cutter Field Road

Directions
From Rt. 3 Exit 5 take Long Pond Road south, and from Rt-3 Exit 3 take Long Pond Road north. At Alden Road turn into the Myles Standish State Forest. After ~ 2 miles turn left onto Upper College Pond Road. After ~3 miles turn left again onto Fearing Pond Road. After a little more than 1 mile stay left onto Circle Drive. Now stay right and get to Cutter Field Road. Turn right and park after about ½ mile in an unpaved area on the left.
Approximate GPS address: Cutter Field Road, Plymouth, Ma 02360

Features
Camp Squanto, at east end of Cutter Field Road. http://www.campsquanto.net/
New Grassy Pond 3 acres, Abner Pond 10 acres, Grassy Pond 3 acres, depth 4 feet, Doctors Pond 2 acres 3 feet deep. Several smaller ponds along the way.

Difficulty
4.4 miles, hilly in places, some fairly long, but not steep.

Hike
Start the hike across the street from the parking area. The trail goes south. Stay right. The pond will be visible on the right. Once you head downhill make a sharp right going northwest. This will lead you to a New Grassy Pond access. To the left of the access there is a great vernal pool. After enjoying both turn around and head south again. Continue till you get to East Line Road (dirt road) Turn right and go over ½ mile. Just before the paved road intersection there is a trail to the left that will take you down to Abner Pond. At the pond make a right and follow around the pond. You will get back to the spot where you came down. Retrace your path and get back to the road. Across the road, just before the paved intersection there is a trail down to Grassy Pond. At the edge of Grassy Pond turn right and then stay left. On the other side turn north, to the bike path and follow it to emerge on Doctors Pond Road. Now follow Doctors Pond Road north. After you reach Doctors Pond on the left, enjoy, and then continue on about 100 feet and take the trail to the right going up. At the top turn right and then left to the edge of a "meadow". Go along the edge and then take the trail going east across the meadow. Go across 5 meadows and 4 patches of forest. Then turn right and head south with the edge of the forest on your left. The trail will emerge very close to the parking area.

New Grassy Pond

Abner Pond

Grassy Pond   Doctors Pond

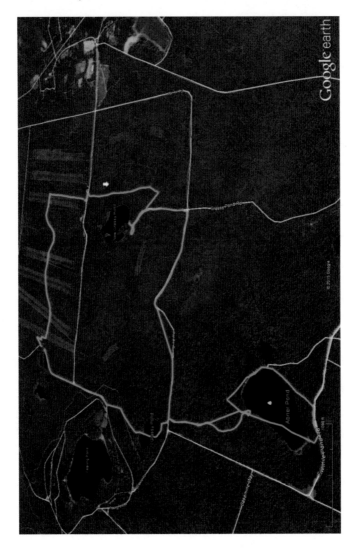

Cutter Filed and Four Pond Trail

Camp Cachalot

Directions
From Rt. 3 Exit 3 or Exit 5 take Long Pond Rd to MSSF East Entrance, Alden Rd. Follow Alden Rd and turn left onto Upper College Road. Now follow signs to Cachalot Camp and Upper College Pond Rd to Fearing Pond Rd 8.5 mi / 15 min. Sharp left onto Fearing Pond Rd, 1.2 mi
Turn right onto SE Line Rd, 0.3 mi. Take the 1st right to stay on SE Line Rd 0.4 mi. Slight left onto Five Mile Pond Rd. Park outside the Camp Entrance. Approximate GPS address, but follow above instructions: Cachalot Scout Reservation, Plymouth, MA 02360

Features
Wooded trails to views of Abner, Five Mile, and Little Long Ponds. Camp Cachalot Scout Camp.

Difficulty
4.8 miles, a few minor hills.

Hike
Walk into the Camp on Five Mile Pond Road. After less than ¼ mile turn left and follow the trail down to Abner Pond and then turn left and follow the trail around the pond. From the east corner take the yellow marker trail back up to the road. Turn right or west and take the next trail on your left, going south. Follow the trail about ¼ mile. It will turn left by a wet area and will then lead you to the main camp area by Five Mile Pond. After passing the camp area the road split. Stay right and follow the trail southwest to Little Long Pond. Turn left and go to the wide sandy path. Turn right and then take the first trail right or north into the forest. At the road turn left again and then right onto SE Line Road. About ½ mile on SE Line road will bring you back to the car.

Abner Pond

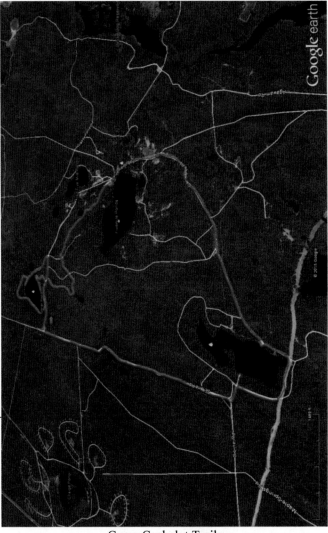

Camp Cachalot Trails

Yellow Trail   Little Long Pond

Frogfoot Brook

Directions
Take Exit 3 off Rt-3. Head towards Long Pond Rd. Turn right After 2 miles turn left onto Alden Rd at the entrance to MSSF. After 1.4 miles turn left onto Upper College Pond Rd. Continue for almost 4 miles, then turn left onto Fearing Pond Rd and then right onto Charge pond Road. The parking lot is about ½ mile on the right.
Approximate GPS address: Charge Pond Rd, Plymouth, MA 02360
Please note that Charge Pond road in the state forest is closed after Labor day. The hike described here starts at the parking lot, which is beyond the gate.

Features
Forest trails, Frogfoot Brook, Frogfoot Brook Reservoir, Makepeace bogs beyond reservoir. A quiet walk in the woods with a beautiful reservoir as a reward.

Difficulty
5.9 miles, mostly flat, but some hills, on narrow sandy roads and wood trails.

Hike
Start the hike by heading south on Charge Pond Road. Make your 3rd right. This will take you over to Wampanoag Road. Turn left and follow it south about ½ mile till you come to a trail head on the right. There are two trails. Take the one sharply to the right. After about a mile the trail emerges on a sandy road turn right and follow the trail. You can shortly take a trail to the brooks edge and along the brook. It does not continue. So, turn around. Once back on the dirt road follow it south to the gas line. It crosses under Frogfoot Reservoir at this point. Just back from the water's edge is a trail that will take you further south to the road that goes across the reservoir dam. Return on the trail through the woods to the gas line and turn right. Follow the gas line for almost a mile. There will be a trail to the left. It is blocked with boulders, but will lead you back to Wampanoag Road. Turn left and follow Wampanoag road till you reach a paved bike trail on the right. Follow it into the campground and then out to Charge Pond Road. Turn left and the parking lot will be to the left off of Charge Pond Road.

Frogfoot Brook   Frogfoot Brook Reservoir

Frogfoot Brook Reservoir   South of Reservoir

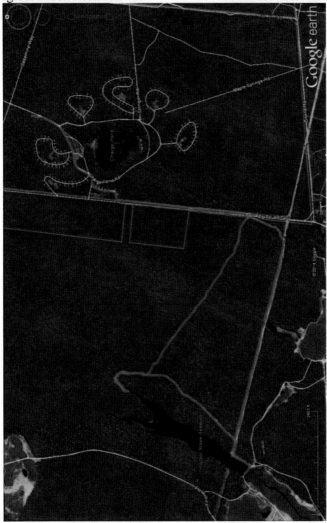

Trail to Frogfoot Reservoir and brook

D. Eastern Area
East Entrance Trails
Directions
From Rt. 3 Exit 5 go towards Long Pond Road. Go about two miles south on Long Pond Road to the entrance of MSSF.
From Rt. 3, Exit 3 go about 3 miles north on Long Pond Road to the entrance of MSSF.
Park in lot on right of entrance.
Approximate GPS address 391 Long Pond Road, Plymouth, MA

Features
Quiet wood trail and sandy road, no special features.
http://www.mass.gov/dcr/parks/southeast/mssf.htm

Difficulty
2.8 miles, many short hills;
3.0miles, many short hills;
3.4 miles, several short hills
4.8 miles, many short hills;

There are 3 hikes in this area. The shortest is 3.1 miles, the blue line. The next on is 3.4 miles, the green line and the longest is 4.8 miles along the perimeter of the others.

Hike 1 (3.0 mile green line)
From Parking lot cross the street and start the hike on the bicycle path. Note the blue trail marker. After about a ½ mile look for the blue trail markers on the right and a trail on the left. Take the trail to the left or east. Follow the infrequent trail markers. The hiking trail marker is blue with an acorn or leaves. There is also a cross-country ski marker. Follow both initially. After about another ½ mile the trail obviously splits. Take the trail to the left and follow it till you can see signs of civilization. After turning almost north the trail will turn south. Follow the trail markers to the right and then make a sharp right turn again away from the road. From here, the trail goes straight for over ½ mile. Just before you see the gate at Alden Road there will be blue markers on the left. Make a right onto the bicycle path at this point and follow it back to the parking lot.

Wintery Trails

Friends Trail; 3.4 miles; blue and purple lines, blue and purple trail marks
From the parking lot cross the street, take the first trail on the left and then look for another trail on your left. Follow the blue trail marks. The trail starts northeasterly, then meanders and finally straight east and then north. Look for purple trail marks on left. Follow purple trail marks back to blue trail (~0.6 miles) turn right. Continue about 1 ½ miles. When you come to a dirt road, turn right/west. Follow it to the next dirt road and turn right again. Now follow it as it gradually turn left and then continues to the bike path. Turn right and follow the bike path to the parking area.

Hike 3: 4.8 miles; red and green lines; perimeter of whole area
From the parking lot cross the street, take the first trail on the left marked with blue blazes, and then look for another trail on your left. The trail meanders around until it is leading south. (Blue trail marks) Continue about 1 ½ miles. When you come to a dirt road, where the blue blazed trail turns right, but you turn left and follow the trail till it is going south and meets Liggett Road. Turn right and follow Liggett Rd all the way to the bike path along Alden Road. Turn right and walk back to the parking area.

Snake Hill/ Gunner's Exchange Hike

Directions
From Rt-3 Exit 5 take Long Pond Road south, and from Rt-3 Exit 3 take Long Pond Road north. At Alden Road turn into the MSSF. After ~ 2 miles make a sharp right onto Snake Hill Road. After ¼ mile park at the intersection of the power lines and Snake Hill Road.
Approximate GPS address: Snake Hill Road, Plymouth, MA

Features
Wooded trails, Gunner's Exchange Pond, Perimeter of Massasoit National Wildlife Refuge

Difficulty
4.5 miles, several short steep hills, narrow trail.

Hike
From the car take the power lines north or to the left. Follow to the large transformer area. Pass to the right of the transformers and then enter the trail on the northeast corner. At the first junction go right and then left. Follow the trail north for almost a mile till it emerges on Snake Hill Road. Turn right and follow the road ¼ mile to a trail on the left. It will take you into a hollow and then over a hill down to Gunner's Exchange Pond. This is the northwest corner of the Massasoit National Wildlife Refuge. Do not go further. The area is closed to the public. There are hefty fines for intruding on the turtles' habitat. Turn around, make your way back to the road, and turn left. After 500 feet there is a gated road to the left. Take it to the first trail on the right. Follow this trail south to the power lines. Turn left and follow the power lines for about 600 feet to a trail on the right before the lines turn. Take the trail south, then east and then meander southwest. When you reach the power lines, look for your car on Snake Hill Road.

Trail to pond

Gunner's Exchange Pond

Snake Hill Trail

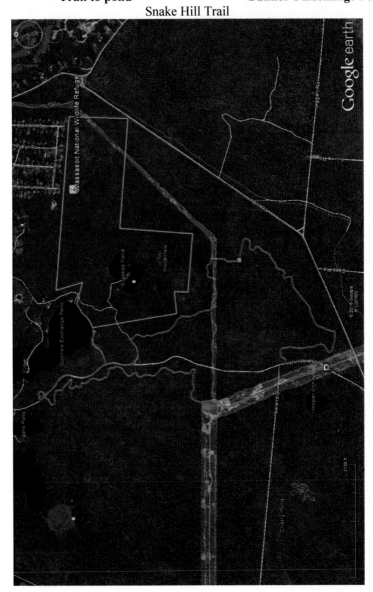

Wing's Hole from Alden Road

Directions

From Exit 3 on Rt. 3 turn west and then right onto Long Pond Rd. MSSF entrance (Alden Rd.) will be in 2 miles on the left. From Rt.3 Exit 5 take Long Pond Rd for 3.7 miles to Entrance of the forest on the right. From entrance go about 1 mile on Alden Rd., and turn left onto Liggett Rd. Park here. Approximate GPS address: Alden Rd, Plymouth, MA 02360

Features

Quit walk in the woods. Turn around point is beautiful Wing's Hole, actually 1 hole with 2 attached smaller holes. Worth the hike.

Difficulty

6.3 miles. Some gentle long hills. Long, but not difficult

Hike

Start by going east on Liggett Rd. for 200 yards. There will be a small trail on the right going south. Follow this weaving trail till you get to Priscilla Rd. Turn left, cross East-Line Rd and look for a trail in about 300 feet on the right. Follow this trail to Three Cornered Pond Rd. Turn left and in 50 feet turn right and follow a trail due west. Once it gets to E-Line Rd. it turn south towards the power lines. Cross the power lines going diagonally to the left. On the other side the small trail continues about 50 feet left of the open area. Follow the trail ~3/4 of a mile south. After it crosses Halfway Pond Rd stay left. At the bottom of the hill there will be an obscure trail to the right leading to Wing's Hole. It is possible to walk/bushwhack around the hole and see the other two side holes. To return take the trail on the right side going north up the hill. At the T near the top of the hill turn left and go to halfway Pond Rd. There go directly across and head north on Cobb Rd. Go Straight 1 ¾ miles on Cobb Rd and the either take the bike path to the right or Alden.
Rd back to Liggett Rd.

Wing's Hole Detail south of Halfway Pond Rd.

Wing's Hole & Saw Pit from Cutter Field Road

Directions
From Rt-3 Exit 5 take Long Pond Road south, and from Rt-3 Exit 3 take Long Pond Road north. At Alden Road turn into the MSSF. After ~ 2 miles turn left onto Upper College Pond Road. After ~3 miles turn left again onto Fearing Pond Road. After a little more than 1 mile stay left onto Circle Drive. Now stay right and get to Cutter Field Road. Turn right and park after about ½ mile in the first paved area on the left. Approximate GPS address: Cutter Field Road, Plymouth, Ma 02360

Features
Cutter Fields are cleared periodically by Mass Wildlife to create habitat for fowl and fowl hunters. They consist of strips of meadow and forest. Saw Pit is a shallow pond with some sandy shore. Wing's Hole is a series of beautiful small ponds strung in a small valley.

Difficulty
3.9 miles, some hills, minimal bushwhacking to Saw Pit.

Hike
Near the northwest corner of the parking area take the trail north. At the first junction make a left and then a right going down the open field. After about 500 feet at the second cross trail turn left again. After ~300 feet take the trail to the right. Follow it to Webster Spring Road. If the continuation of the trail is not straight across from you, turn left, go about 100 feet and turn onto the trail on your right. Follow this trail about a mile till it starts turning right, follow the turn, and come to a T. Turn left go about 150 feet. When you come to the taller trees turn right and follow that trail till you can see Saw Pit on your left. Find a convenient clearer area and make your way down to the water. Now go left and follow the shore around. When you get to the open area near the southern end turn left and go about 100feet directly east to the trail that led you to the pond. Turn right or west on the trail and retrace your steps back to the taller trees. At the junction stay right and take the trail through the woods to Briggs Road. Cross and continue north. When the trail makes a sharp right continue up the hill. Past the top look for a lesser trail on your left. Follow it northwest to Wing Hole. Up and down the valley from the major hole there are several smaller water areas you might want to explore. Now head back south east the way you came. At the junction turn right and follow this trail to Briggs Road. Cross and continue. At the first junction bear right. At the next junction you can stay right and retrace your steps back to the car, or you can go straight/south. There will be a sharp left and then bear right and heads south to Webster Spring Road. On the road go a few steps to your right and the take the trail to your left heading south along the edge of the field. After about ¼ mile turn left into the woods. Then take the first trail right. At the second cross trail make a quick left and then right. The car will be straight ahead.

Saw Pit and Wing's Hole from Cutter Field Road

Saw Pit   Wing's Hole

E- Line Rd from Mast Rd

Directions

Long way, but half a smooth ride: From Rt.3 Exit 3 go west towards Long Pond Road. Make a right on Long Pond Road and go about two miles till you get to Mast Road on your left. Turn onto Mast Road and follow it just past the power lines and the entrance to the Girls Scout camp. There will be a Wildlands trust parking area on your right.

Or,

Smoother ride: From Rt. 3 Exit 3 turn east towards Long Pond Road. Turn left on Long Pond Road. Go about 2 miles, turn right onto Halfway Pond Road. Follow it till it splits into Wareham Rd to the left and Mast Road to the right. Take Mast Road and follow it along the edge of the pond. After about 1 ½ miles turn left and find a Wildlands Trust parking area on the left.

Approximate GPS street address 500 Mast Rd, Plymouth, MA

GPS: 498 Gallows Pond Rd, 02360

Features

Mast Road, Three Cornered Pond Road, E-Line Road, Half Way Pond, Cattle Pond. Quiet walk in the woods, forest roads, and an old overgrown trail.

Difficulty

4.6 miles, some minor hills.

Hike

Hike 1. Take the trail on the south side of the parking area. Follow it uphill to the junction and turn right. You are now on the Gramp's Loop Trail. Go west for about ½ mile. Just before the trail makes a sharp left take a small winding trail over to Three Cornered Pond Road. Turn left. Stay left as a trail separates parallel to Three Cornered Pond Road. Follow it to E-Line Road. Turn left or south. Go 1 mile, cross the power lines, and when the road makes a 45 degree turn to the left follow it. After the turn look for a small trail to the left. Do not take that one. Continue on E-Line Rd to the bottom of the gradual hill. On the south side of the little valley take a well-defined trail east or left. Continue east to the power lines. Cross and then look for a continuation maybe 100 yards to the right and just before the hill leading up to the power lines Continue on the trail till you see a house ahead .Turn left here. And then left again on a dirt road which will take you to the shore of Cattle Pond. At the pond turn right and follow the shore line even though the road disappears. There is a trail, soggy at times, but it will bring you out on a dirt road, which shortly brings you to Agawam Rd. Turn left and follow Agawam Rd to Mast Road. Now turn left again and follow Mast road along the pond and then north to the cars.

Mast Rd to MSSF E-Line Rd to Cattle Pond Trail

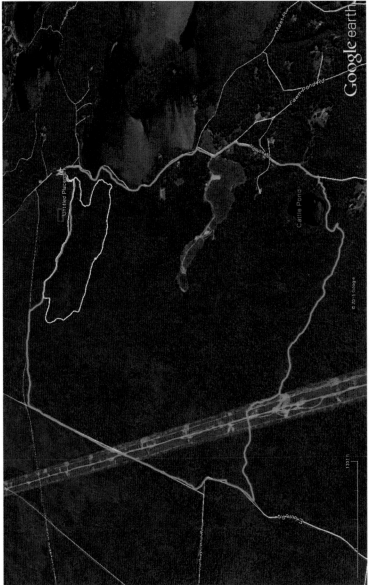

Index

Abner Pond, 50, 52

Around College Pond, 6

Bare Hill, 16, 20, 28, 32, 34, 36, 40

Barrett Pond, 6, 11, 42, 43

Bentley Loop, 6, 14

Camp Cachalot, 6, 52, 53

Camp Squanto, 46, 50

Cattle Pond, 64, 65

Charge Pond, 6, 46, 47, 48, 54

Cherry Pond, 6, 18, 19

Cherry Pond Valley, 6, 18, 19

Cobb Rd, 60

Cranford Road, 11, 12

Curlew Pond, 6, 28, 32, 34

Curlew Pond Road, 28, 32

Cutter Field, 6, 50, 62, 63

Cutter Fields, 62

Docs Ponds, 6

Doctors Pond, 46, 50, 51

E- Line Rd, 64

East Entrance, 6, 24, 52, 56

East Head Reservoir, 6, 7, 10, 11, 22, 24, 25

E-Line Road, 6, 64

Fearing Pond, 6, 11, 24, 46, 47, 50, 52, 54, 62

Federal Cranberry Bogs, 34

Federal Furnace Road, 12, 18

Federal Pond, 6, 7, 16, 34, 35, 36, 37

Fire Tower, 6, 16, 17, 20, 21

Five Mile Pond, 52

Fivemile Pond, 52

Forest Headquarters, 16, 24, 26

Frogfoot Brook, 6, 54, 55

Garmin, 5

Grady Pond, 6, 44

Gramp's Loop, 64

Grassy Pond, 46

Gunner's Exchange Hike, 58

Halfway Pond, 22

Howland Road, 11, 12, 18

Jessup Road, 42

Kamesit Way, 16

Little Long Pond, 52, 53

Little Widgeon Pond, 6, 30, 31

Lost Horse Bog, 6, 38, 39, 40, 41

Lunxus Rd, 42

Manters Hole, 7, 28, 32

Massasoit National Wildlife Refuge, 4, 58

Mast Road, 64

Negas Road, 26

Negus Road, 14

New Grassy Pond, 50

New Long Pond, 11

Northwest Corner, 28

Plymouth, 1, 2

Rocky Pond, 6, 32, 34, 35, 36, 37

Round Pond, 22

Ryan Road, 38, 40

Sabbatia Road, 20

Saw Pit, 6, 62, 63

Shady Acres, 6, 40, 41

Shoestring Road, 40

Snake Hill, 6, 11, 12, 58, 59

Three Cornered Pond, 22, 23

Torrey Pond, 6, 11, 16, 20, 21

Wampanoag, 10, 54

Wampanog Road, 54

Wayout Road, 11, 16, 18

Webster Spring Road, 62

Wing Holes, 6, 60

Made in the USA
Middletown, DE
17 October 2020